T0341665

Living room on upper floor, ca. 1933.

…g area in the yard.

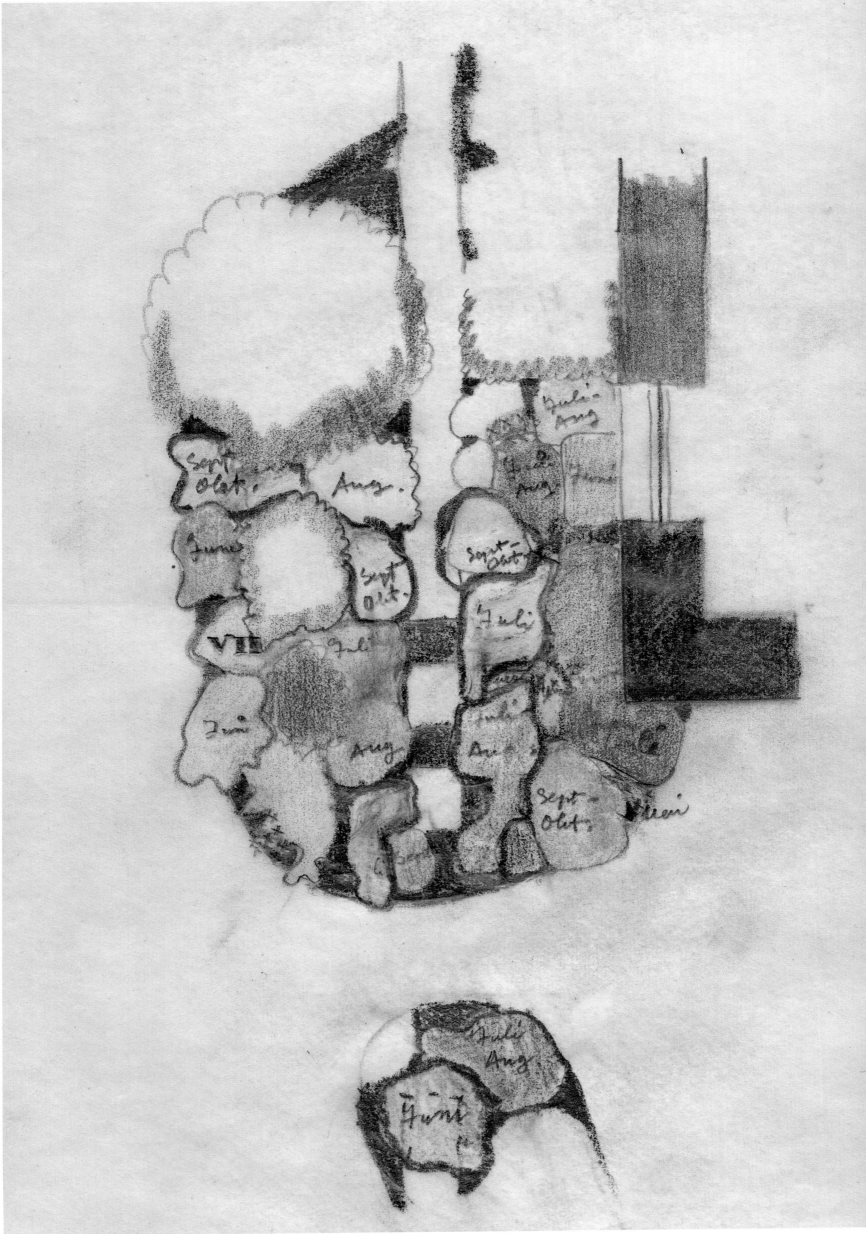

Sketch of plants at the southwest corner of the house with information on blooming times. Rudolf Olgiati, 1951.

Jahr : 1937
Standort : Berner Rosen
Ausmass : 1:8.25   3.5 × 8 m25 =
M. : 1:50
Angelegt Herbst 1937.35

Erdbeen
Erdbeeren
ges.
Sept. 36
=RDBEEREN
1.00

0.30   0.25

19.V.37

Buschbohnen
BUSCHBOHNEN

4.65

Berner Rosen

1.20
30 cm

RÜBEN
Neuauise
verbessert

G R
19.V.37

Rosen
15 × 14
versetzt
Okt. 1937

0.90

Früh-
Kartoffeln
Selbe
Sorte
20.V.37

2.70   2.50

1:8.25

20.V.37

Erträge:
Rübensäen : gute   versetzt Okt. 1936 satt
Rosen : versetzt Herbst Okt. 1936 satt.
Phlox : versetzt Okt. 1936 satt.
Rüben : Neuauise verbessert 12 kg nicht
Früh Kartoffeln, Selbe Sorte

ch of vegetable garden by Rudolf Olgiati.

Garden floor hall with the garden library, the Grisons library, and enlarged photographs of the chapel at St. Johann Monastery in Müstair and Tarasp Castle.

Rudolf Olgiati's collection of cultural artifacts in the barn. Throughout his life Rudolf Olgiati collected and inventoried old objects from Grisons, intending to "save them from bad times."
The enlargement of a 1655 pen-and-ink drawing by Jan Hackaert in the village of Flims in obre pont (Flims in the Grey League).

ction of cultural artifacts. The walls of the former barn were whitewashed.

ction of cultural artifacts. The barn contained approximately three thousand objects.

…ance to the Rudolf Olgiati House, ground floor. The early eighteenth-century door came from a demolished house in the historical part of Flims.

Kitchen entrance. The arch was added in 1968.

en. The seventeenth-century walnut chair at the head of the table comes from South Grisons and has been branded with the marks "BIM" and "B+M."

crete stairway to the upper floor and entrance to the architectural office. The secretary sat at the desk in the background.

Meeting area in the architectural office. Rudolf Olgiati drank tea with his clients in front of the stone stove. He designed it and the white furniture himself. The plans on the table show his hou

in the northern bedroom on the upper floor. The Gothic bas-relief of Saint Barbara has been carved out of linden wood.

Living room.

g room with private desk.

Rudolf Olgiati's bedroom. A map of Grisons hangs on the wall, and there is a movable book holder in front for large illustrated editions. The sixteenth-century gabled chest in the foreground ce

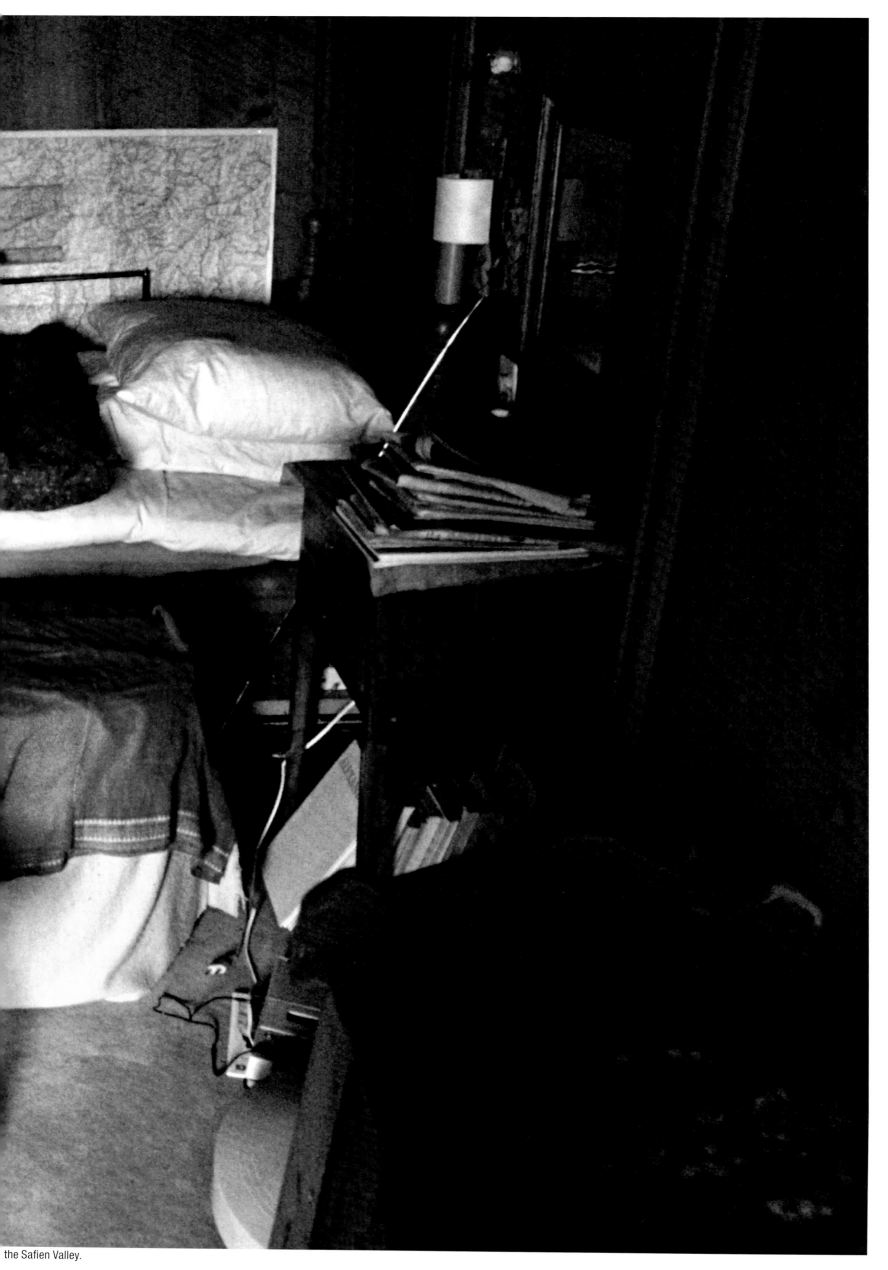

the Safien Valley.

The Dado estate, built and inhabited
by Rudolf Olgiati between 1931 and 1995.
Site plan with garden level 1/100.

1 Garage
2 Garden floor hall
3 Storage cellar with oil tanks
4 Utility room
5 Cloakroom
6 Bath / toilet
7 Kitchen with dining table
8 Architectural office with meeting area
9 Archives with photocopier
10 Living room
11 Bedroom
12 Guestroom
13 Children's bedroom
14 Storage room
15 Archives
16 Barn with collection of cultural artifacts

☐ Private
■ Work

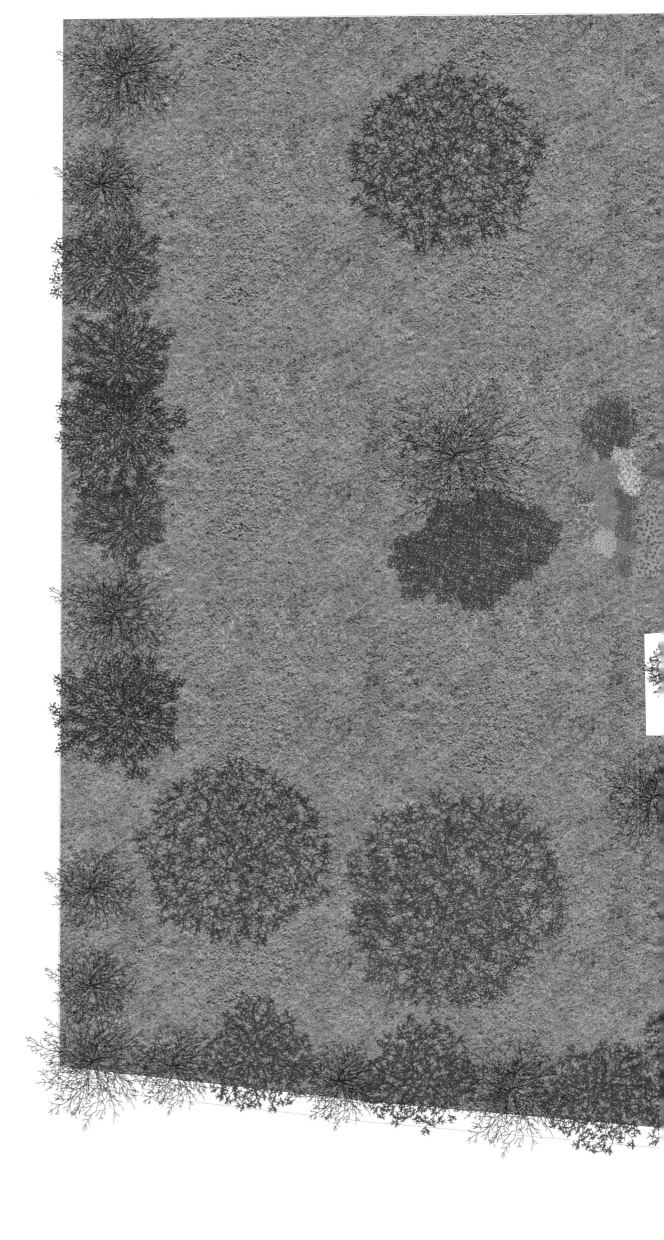

Ground floor 1/100.

1 Garage
2 Garden floor hall
3 Storage cellar with oil tanks
4 Utility room
5 Cloakroom
6 Bath / toilet
7 Kitchen with dining table
8 Architectural office with meeting area
9 Archives with photocopier
10 Living room
11 Bedroom
12 Guestroom
13 Children's bedroom
14 Storage room
15 Archives
16 Barn with collection of cultural artifacts

☐ Private
■ Work

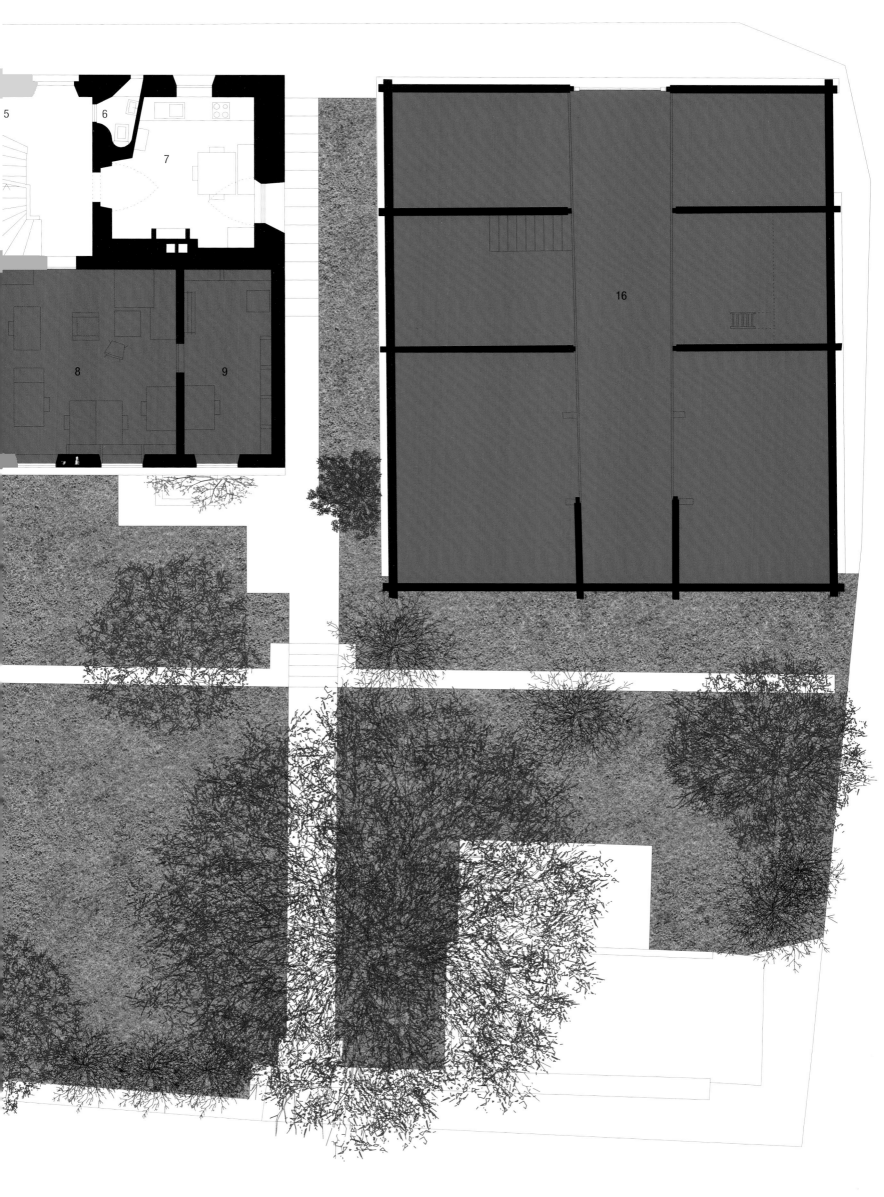

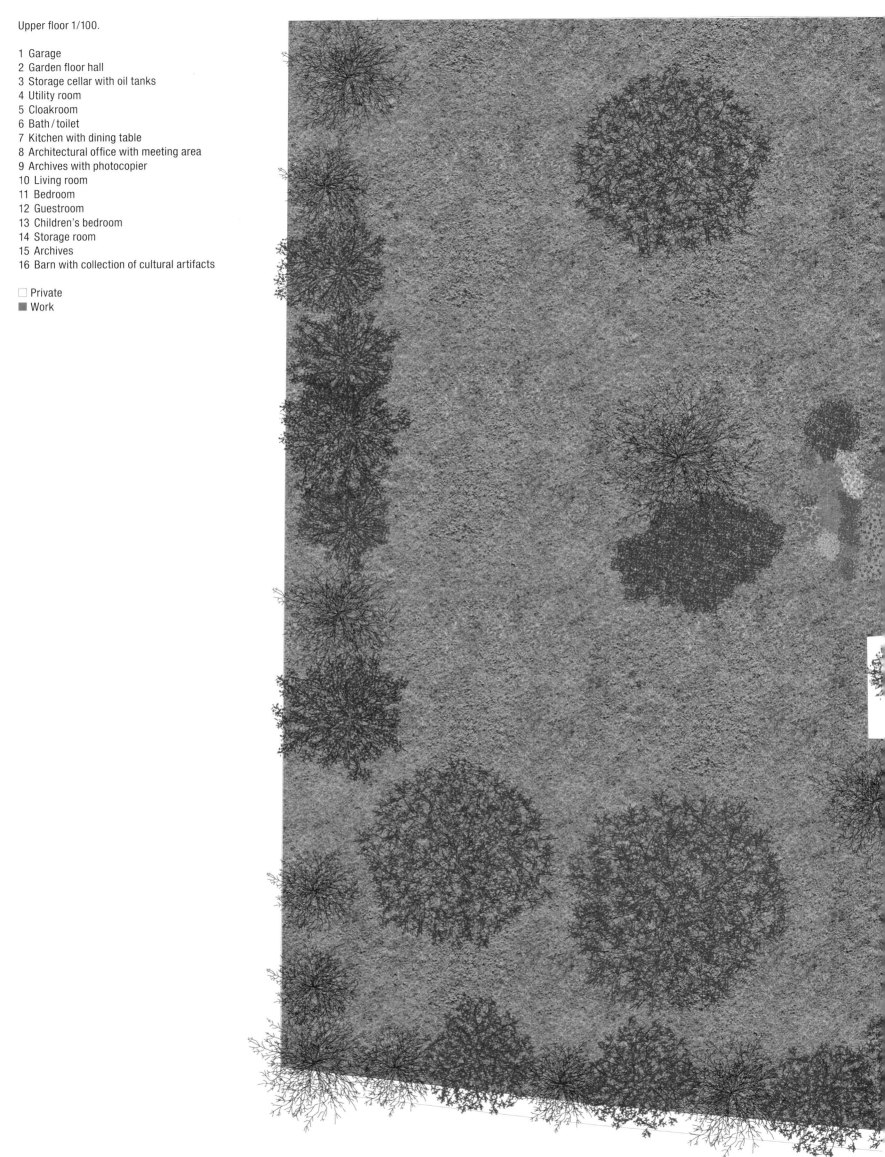

Upper floor 1/100.

1 Garage
2 Garden floor hall
3 Storage cellar with oil tanks
4 Utility room
5 Cloakroom
6 Bath / toilet
7 Kitchen with dining table
8 Architectural office with meeting area
9 Archives with photocopier
10 Living room
11 Bedroom
12 Guestroom
13 Children's bedroom
14 Storage room
15 Archives
16 Barn with collection of cultural artifacts

☐ Private
■ Work

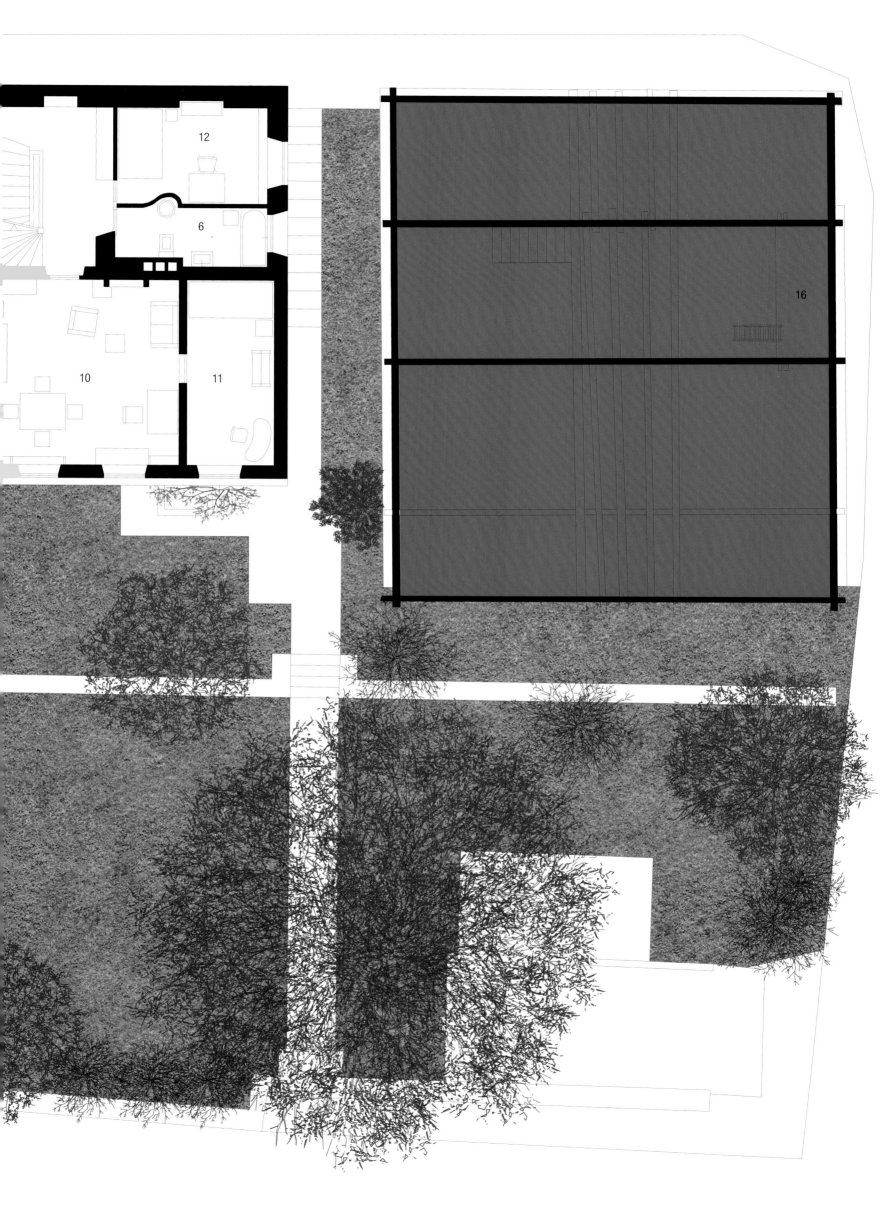

Attic 1/100.

☐ Private
■ Work

Site plan, Flims, 1/6000, with the Olgiati property marked in red in the "Dado" quarter. "Dado" means "outside" in Romansh and refers to the outer edge of the historical village.

Dado—Built and Inhabited by Rudolf Olgiati and Valerio Olgiati

The Olgiati family's estate is located in the Dado section of Flims (Dado is Romansh for "outside" and refers to the outer edge of the village). Rudolf Olgiati acquired the house from his family in 1931 and implemented his architectural ideas in it throughout his life. Valerio Olgiati inherited the property after his father's death and built an architectural office on the site of the barn. This book not only documents the architectural alterations, but also shows how architecture and home décor are an expression of the inhabitants' culture. The question of cultural influence is of special interest in this context since it is not only determined by upbringing, but also by individual experience and volition. Dado is a site where this interaction has taken place. The present situation shows Valerio Olgiati's relationship with his father's architectural and cultural legacy.

Rudolf Olgiati, personal details: 1910 born the son of Oreste Olgiati and Agnes Parli. 1934 architectural degree at the ETH, Zurich, under Prof. Otto Rudolf Salvisberg. 1935–1937 several stays in Rome. 1938–1939 architectural office in Zurich. From 1944 architectural office in Flims. 1995 death in Flims.
Property details: 1931 Rudolf Olgiati acquires the Dado estate from the Parli family together with his brother Guido. 1931–1995 ongoing alterations of the Dado house. Rudolf collects and inventories cultural artifacts in the barn. 1935 first major remodeling. 1948 sole acquisition of the property. 1968 major remodeling, which forms the basis of the house's current design.

Valerio Olgiati, personal details: 1958 born the son of Rudolf Olgiati and Irene Canova in Chur. 1986 architectural degree at the ETH, Zurich, under Fabio Reinhart. 1988–1993 architectural office in Zurich. 1993–1995 stay in Los Angeles. 1996 architectural office in Zurich. Since 2008 architectural office with Tamara Olgiati in Flims. 1994–2005 guest lecturer in Switzerland, Germany, England, and the United States. Since 2002 full professor at the Accademia di Architettura Mendrisio. 2009 Professor at Harvard University (Kenzo Tange Chair).
Property details: 1999: sole acquisition of Dado from the estate of Rudolf Olgiati. 2007/2008: a new office building is erected to replace the barn.

Colophon
This book was published in conjunction with the exhibition "Dado—Built and Inhabited by Rudolf Olgiati and Valerio Olgiati," running from December 13, 2009, to April 11, 2010 in DAS GELBE HAUS FLIMS.
Editor: Selina Walder, Creative Director: Dino Simonett, Graphic Design: Bruno Margreth, Lithography: Pascal Werner, Cronica, Chur; Printmanagement Plitt GmbH, Oberhausen, Translation: Adam Blauhut, Printing and Binding: Kösel GmbH & Co. KG, Altusried-Krugzell. Printed in Germany.

Library of Congress Control Number: 2009938747

Cover: Marble plaque. Entrance to the Valerio Olgiati House. Back cover: marble plaque. Entrance to the Rudolf Olgiati House. Opposite photo: Dado in winter 2009

Photo credits: Archive Valerio Olgiati (front cover, 12, 16/17, 34/35, 55−73, 76−83, Bettina Rogosky 14/15, 32/33), gta Archiv/ETH Zurich: Rudolf Olgiati Papers (2−11, 13, 16, 20−31, Photographer: anonymous, Hajo Willig 8−10, 16, 21−31), Christian Kerez (17, 19), Selina Walder (45, 75), David Grandorge (84), Fabrizio Ballabio (86/87), Dino Simonett (back cover). Legends and plans: Selina Walder

© 2010 Birkhäuser Verlag AG. Basel · Boston · Berlin. P.O. Box 133, CH-4010 Basel, Switzerland.
Part of Springer Science + Business Media
Printed on acid-free paper produced from chlorine-free bleached pulp. TCF ∞

ISBN: 978-3-0346-0430-7
987654321 www.birkhauser.ch

The Dado estate, built and inhabited
by Valerio Olgiati since 1999.
Site plan and garden level 1/100.

1 Garage / carport
2 Garden floor hall
3 Wine cellar
4 Storage room
5 Cloakroom
6 Bath / toilet
7 Kitchen
8 Dining room
9 Library and private office
10 Living room
11 Bedroom
12 Dressing room
13 Guestroom
14 Storage room
15 Utility room and archives
16 Architectural office
17 Meeting room

☐ Private
■ Work

Ground floor 1/100.

1 Garage / carport
2 Garden floor hall
3 Wine cellar
4 Storage room
5 Cloakroom
6 Bath / toilet
7 Kitchen
8 Dining room
9 Library and private office
10 Living room
11 Bedroom
12 Dressing room
13 Guestroom
14 Storage room
15 Utility room and archives
16 Architectural office
17 Meeting room

☐ Private
■ Work

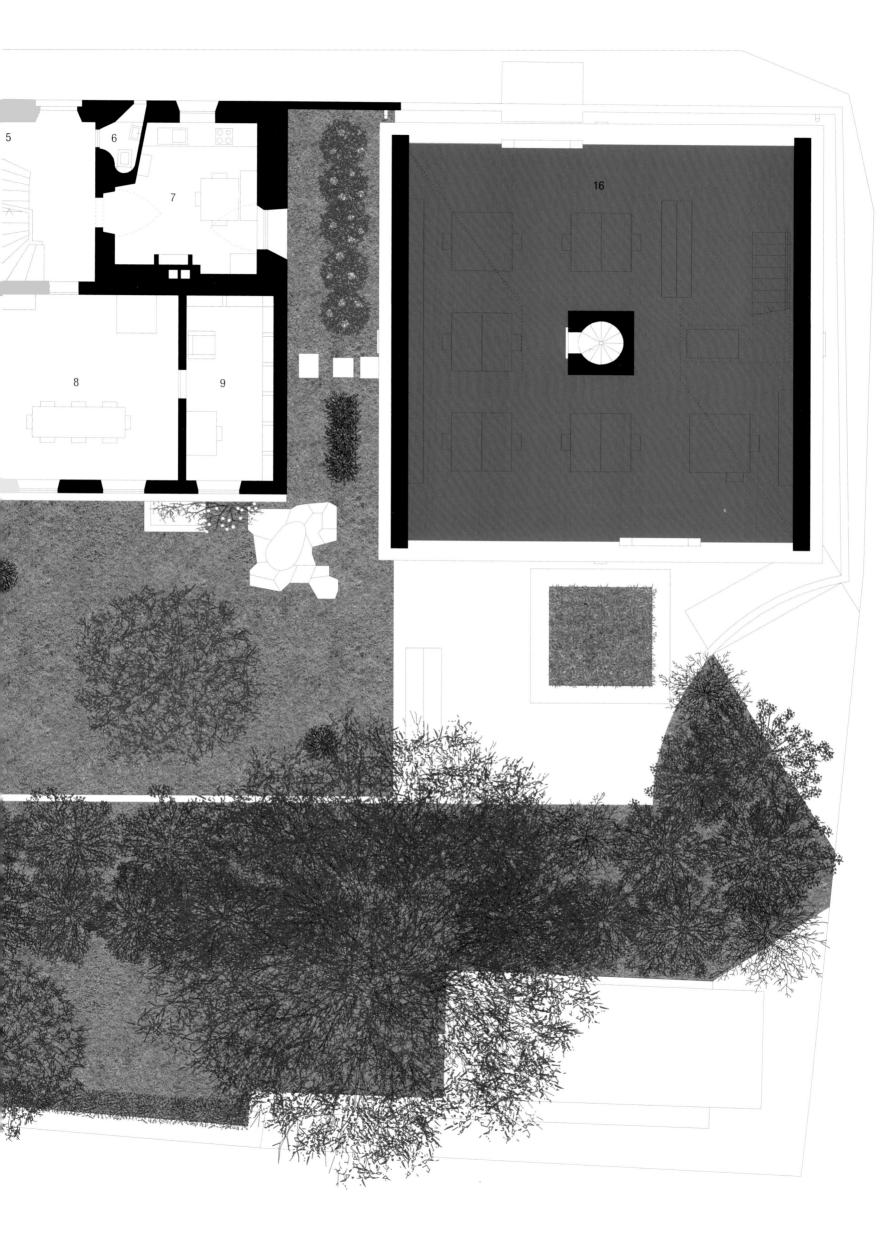

Upper floor 1/100.

1 Garage / carport
2 Garden floor hall
3 Wine cellar
4 Storage room
5 Cloakroom
6 Bath / toilet
7 Kitchen
8 Dining room
9 Library and private office
10 Living room
11 Bedroom
12 Dressing room
13 Guestroom
14 Storage room
15 Utility room and archives
16 Architectural office
17 Meeting room

☐ Private
■ Work

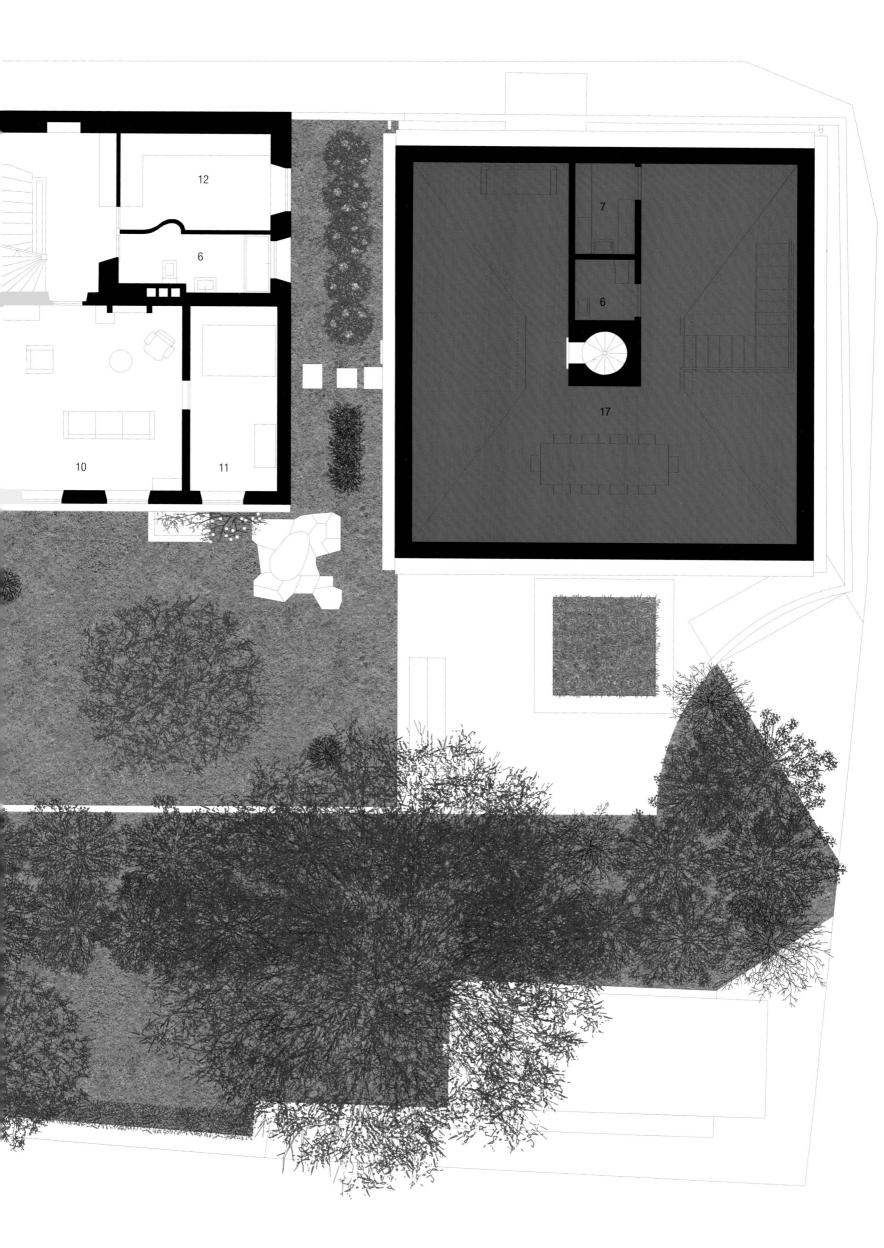

Attic 1/100.

1 Garage / carport
2 Garden floor hall
3 Wine cellar
4 Storage room
5 Cloakroom
6 Bath / toilet
7 Kitchen
8 Dining room
9 Library and private office
10 Living room
11 Bedroom
12 Dressing room
13 Guestroom
14 Storage room
15 Utility room and archives
16 Architectural office
17 Meeting room

☐ Private
■ Work

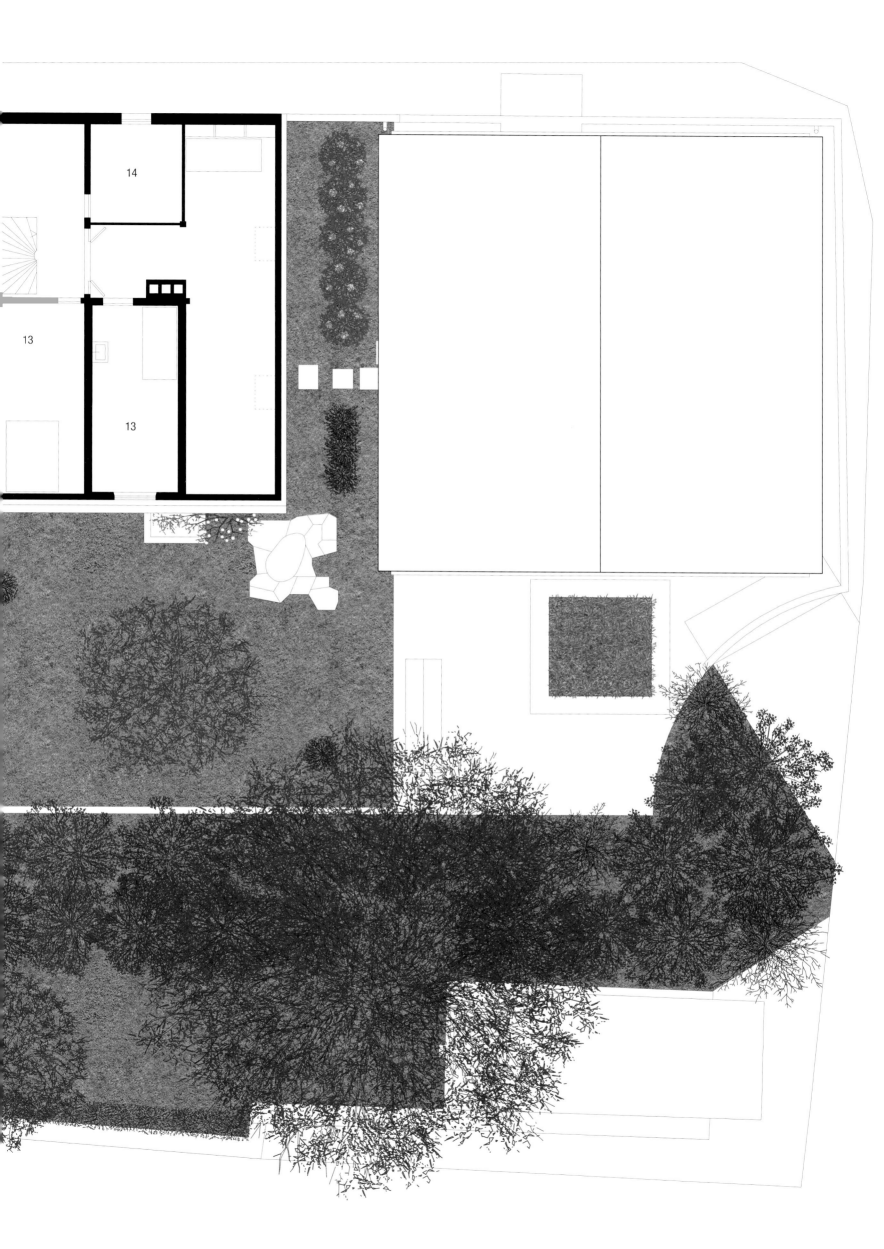

io Olgiati's bedroom. A framed photograph of "Cuadra San Cristóbal" by Luis Barragán is hanging on the wall, photographer: René Burri.

Living room. Tamara and Valerio Olgiati brought the carpet back from Morocco.

Wooden icon, anonymous nineteenth-century Amerindian painting from Peru. The Mother of God and Mother Earth are combined in one figure.

Stairway leading to the upper floor with an enlarged photograph of the Fatehpur Sikri. Fox bag designed by Tamara Olgiati, and the couple's cat Subaru.

...ry with books belonging to Rudolf Olgiati and Valerio Olgiati.

Private desk in library. The golden frame holds a picture of Valerio's father, Rudolf, and mother, Irene. The Polaroid shows his wife, Tamara, and there is a rendering of a project in Albania belo

Dining room. Valerio Olgiati designed the table.

An Inca stone weapon, a lamp by Isamu Noguchi, and a model of the Sari d'Orcino House in Corsica stand on the stone stove in the dining room.

entrance and fireplace.

Kitchen. The miniature on the fireplace depicts three women in the middle of an Islamic garden.

Garden floor hall.

Olgiati's office in summer 2009. The pool is heat-insulated and contains exotic lilies.

"Carport."

area.

Desk 17 in the architectural office. Normal state – orderly.

Ground floor.

floor with a view of the Senda Stretga.

Upper floor with meeting room.

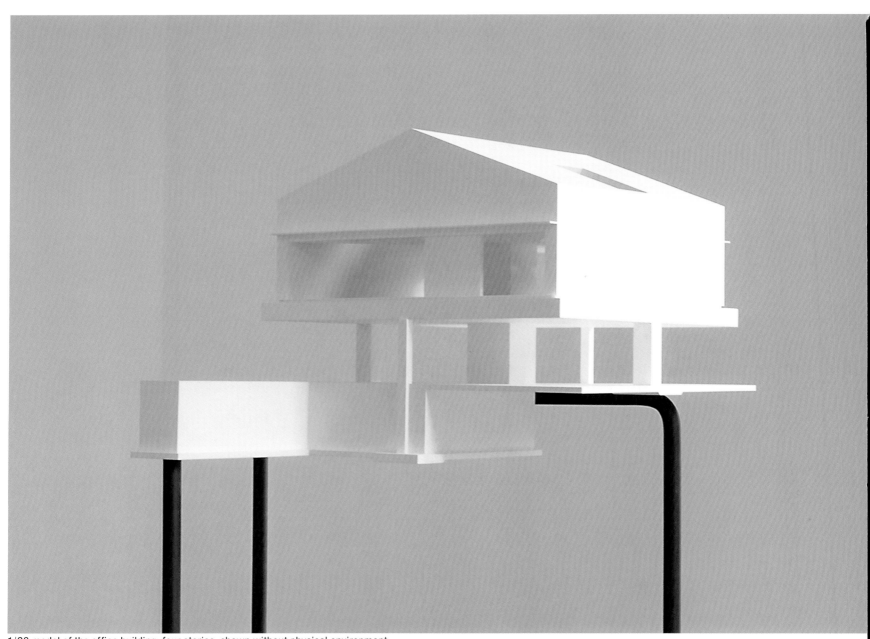

1/20 model of the office building, four stories, shown without physical environment.

View of Senda Stretga 1.